Twice Broken

Twice Broken

Poetry by Sharon Harris

A publication of the
Jackpine Writers' Bloc, Inc.
Menahga, Minnesota

Published by
The Jackpine Writers' Bloc
13320 149th Ave
Menahga, Minnesota 56464
sharrick1@wcta.net
www.sharonharrispoetry.com

Printed in the United States of America

Cover and book design
by Tarah L. Wolff

ISBN: 978-1-928690-43-6

Often a person has a heartbreak that
impacts their whole life.

In my life, I have been

Twice Broken . . .

Two Great Loves

you two,
you two great loves
of my life
where are you now?

you each took a big chunk
out of the center of my life,
took the heart and soul of me
and you both left me
here alone

false promises on your tongues
no staying power
you stole me away from everything
safe and solid
took me for long whimsical rides
for years
with no promise of longevity
where are you now?

I let you do it
encouraged you
believed in you
my soft heart was no match
for either of you
with your worldly ways
the things you said
lies twisting through your words

as I grow old and alone
when I am lonely and longing
where are you now?

Acknowledgments

Grateful acknowledgment is made to the following magazines and
journals for the previous publication of these poems:

American Anthology of Poetry: "Hurt Enough," "When You Are
Near"
American Poetry Anthology: "Bright Promises"
CSS Publications: "Bittersweet," "Smiling"
Fine Arts Press: "Currents," "Sorrows"
For Poets Only: "Alive," "My Meaning"
Green Valley Publishing: "Rainbow"
Lake Region Review: "Heartfull, Hurtful" (published as "Two Hearts")
Lucidity: "Things"
Moccasin: "Secrets," "Together"
Nashville Newsletter: "Delicate Images"
New Worlds Unlimited: "Outwardly and Inwardly," "Tangled," "Today"
Newsletter Inago: "Illusion"
P & S Publishing: "Island"
Poetry Magazine: "Limbo"
Poetry Press: "My Need"
Poets at Work: "Escape," "Hurting," "Since Time Began"
Potpourri International Publishing: "My Life"
Quill Books: "Music and Light," "Shining Moment"
Shining Waters Press: "Fade Away," "Touch the Edge of You"
Submit: "Never the Same," "Survive," "Your Mark"
Suwanee Poetry: "Old Promises"
Talking Stick: "Abstract Painting of My Dark Outlaw," "Another Life,"
"Another Person's Memories," "Decisions, Decisions," "The
Empty End of Things," "Keep Busy," "Mindful Meal," "Now I
Can Feel," "Observations," "The Same Stars," "Things I Fear,"
"Touch," "Weekend River Walk," "Will You Know?"
Ursus Press: "Everything"
Wide Open: "New Things"
Yellow Butterfly: "Brief Light," "A Lifetime," "My Heart Hangs
Heavy," "Remembering"
Yesterday, Today & Dreams: "Velvet Haze"

POETRY BOOKS BY SHARON HARRIS

Timeless Tracks
Life Savors
Unspoken

Table of Contents
FANTASY
(for P.)

Table of Contents
FANTASY
(for P.)

Table of Contents
STOLEN HEART
(for R.)

Table of Contents
STOLEN HEART
(for R.)

Twice Broken

FANTASY

(for P.)

Before

Bright Promises

I wish you could know
how much I want you.
I wish I could tell you
that when you touch me
as a friend
you stir me so deeply
that every inch of me trembles.

I wish you could know
the depths of me
and I would like to reach
all those bright promises
that hide in your eyes
but you are not mine
and never can be

so I will never know . . .
you will never know . . .

Limbo

I am held here in limbo
between the two of you,
knowing I must stay with him,
knowing he is all the safety
and security I so desperately need,
knowing he is necessary
to my well-planned life.

but then there's you—
you with all your excitement
how can I turn you away
before I've really touched you
how can I turn away
from your knowing smile
and curling hair
how can I say no
to the broad strength
of your hands
and the skill of your fingers
how can I say no
to your desire
and to mine . . .

My Need

you made me need you and want you,
you know,
and I am afraid that my need
is greater than yours.

I am afraid that the pain
I see glistening in your eyes
is not real.
it is only a reflection
of my own.

Unmentioned

the kiss
we shared
remains
unmentioned

hovering there
between us
lurking in my
downcast eyelashes

whispering
some secrets
in the words
we don't breathe
into the space
between us

aching
to be discussed
yearning to
happen again

wondering
and imagining
what else
there is
to discover

knowing
we each
have other lives
other commitments

wanting to be
irresponsible
but knowing
that we can't

During

Alive

I'm alive! I'm alive!
I must remind myself
over and over
that I'm alive
no matter how dead I feel inside
when you're not here.

A Beautiful Dream

sometimes
I think
you have just been
a beautiful dream,
a figment
of my imagination,
my fantasy come true

the sight of you
is haunting me always
elusive as mist
like frost gleaming momentarily
in sunshine

but mostly
I know you are real
more real
than all the rest
of my life

your hands
have branded
my body with touches
your words
are written clearly
all through my memory

you have engraved
your name
on my soul

Brief Light

today you are all I can see
in the endless rush
of people and thoughts and ideas
that pass through my days.

is it possible
is it conceivable
that someday I will lose you?
that someday you may mean
no more to me
than a shooting star
means to the whole night sky?

is it possible
is it conceivable
that you are only
a brief flickering light
in the whole long darkness
of my existence?

Currents

you
touched my life.
at first you were like soft sunshine
gently warming my skin with your presence.
you came like easy ripples
across my clear untroubled pool
of consciousness.

but then,
without warning,
you dove quickly, deeply
into the calm unruffled waters of my life,
sending wicked wild waves
rolling across me.

you
awakened things in me
I did not know were there.
you changed the surfaces of me entirely.
and now
I do not know,
I cannot remember,
a time before these storms came,
before you sent these restless,
ever-changing currents
sweeping across the depths of me.

Delicate Images

feel this feeling.
touch this thought.
savor the damp air washing over you
like a splash of water.
remember the scent of grass,
the design of trees against the sky,
the pattern of wild flowers along the trail,
the feel of rain on your face.

hold this, remember this,
the sights, the sounds, the movements;
keep these delicate images
pressed in your memory;
keep them, add to them.

go on all the way through life
collecting treasures,
seeking glad moments,
making memories,
for your old age.

Empty Heart

I thought I was over you
and moving on

today, seeing you on the street,
you flashed that grin

and blindsided me

my empty heart
filled up again

Escape

escape
how I long for escape
from this dreary body
and dreary life

I want to drift away
I want for just a moment
to recapture the stillness
the utter peace
and precious ease
of movement
unfettered by my heavy body

I dimly remember
my between-life states
floating free of pain
merging with my friends and loves
merging mind and soul
not just body

I want this back
even for just a moment

how can I
recapture it?
I almost can
with drugs or drink
or when I'm loving you—
almost I can touch it!—
almost!

Everything

my favorite time of day
my favorite time of year
early evening in early spring
long shadows slide soothingly
across gorgeous, green grasses
winds whisper golden secrets
to me.

I am afraid.
I have everything in life
right now
that I have ever wanted.

I am afraid.
where can I go from here
but down?
what can I do from here
but lose?

Fade Away

sometimes the sharp edge of reality
is too much for people.

they must escape
even temporarily
by the dulling touch of drugs
or with the slightly paralyzing effect
of liquor to their minds.

I used to drink in the tang of life
and relish each sound, each moment.

but was I really living then?
or was I merely existing in my easy,
boring, comfortable life?

now I want to fade away.
I have known pain.
I want to step back from the harsh light
of reality.
I want to hide and muffle the sharp sounds
of existence.

I want to just drift painlessly,
slightly out of touch,
through the troubles
I have created for myself.

Hurt Enough

I have
hurt enough
over you

to last
a thousand
lifetimes

Hurting

I never imagined
how much I could physically hurt
just because I can't touch you.

I crave your hands upon me,
I want to feel your hands upon my back
pulling me down to you.

I never imagined
withdrawal symptoms from you
could be so bad.

Illusion

since I met you
I've been caught in a dream
and I can't wake up
my life has been confused and dazed
I'm always lost in thought,
slowly whirling in my mind,
turning lazy circles in ever-
widening patterns
of kaleidescoping colors

I see only you
the rest is a hazy illusion
the rest is soft focus
voices are muted
you are all I hear
you are all I know
you are all I have left

everything else is far away and dim
and really doesn't matter
at all

Island

I don't want
to lose you
in this ocean of pain
and storm
of circumstances

I don't want you
swept from me
by interfering currents
of people
and pressures

we've drifted too far apart
and I can't reach you
I can't possibly touch you
I must strain
just to keep you in sight

all I can do is give you space
and follow you through lashing waves
and wait breathlessly, silently
and hope there will be an island,
a break in the storm,
calmer waters where I can join you—
an oasis of pleasure in the sun
somewhere in our future . . .

A Lifetime

I feel like
I have not
seen you
for a year

or
touched you
for a
lifetime

Music and Light

the music is gone from my life;
it left with you.
I saw you tuck it under your arm
and take it with you
along with the sun,
and all the passion I'd ever known
and all the pleasure
and excitement.

you shut off the lights
and closed the door on me
leaving me locked
in the cold rooms of my mind
filled only with a silence and darkness
with lonely scattered memories
flickering
like lost fireflies
at the window.

My Heart Hangs Heavy

my heart
hangs heavy and low today
like it was made of lead.
it hurts me.

I need so much to touch you.
I need to stretch my arms
out to you
and just touch the tips
of your fingers
with my own
and feel the electricity of you
flashing through my veins
reminding me
refreshing me
giving me strength
to go on . . .

My Meaning

you
are my center,
my reason,
my
meaning

Never the Same

our souls
touched
and touched
again

and were
never the same
after
the touching

New Things

you enlarged my life
you widened my horizons
you opened me
to new things
previously
unimagined

Old Promises

there's nothing worse
than being held in one place,
trapped by old promises,
by people and past choices,

and wanting
so much
to be
somewhere
else . . .

Outwardly and Inwardly

outwardly
I smile.
I walk along cheerfully
through my days
and do my work
and say all the right things.

inwardly
I am weeping.
I can hardly function;
the days are so long;
I cannot concentrate
on anything
but you.

Rainbows

there is such an emptiness in me
when you're not here
and I start to fear that
we are wrong to do this.
come fill me with your warmth
and give me comfort.
come dazzle me
with your presence.

when you are with me
I know without a doubt
that we are right
and we belong together.

and when you must go again
please leave me with some
of your crystal words
to hang in the air around me
to shine rainbows
around my small dark world
to hold me together
till I can see you again.

Secrets

tears brim up in my eyes
threatening to overflow

like the secrets
filling me up inside
threatening to burst out
in foolish words
upon my tongue

Shining Moment

looking back
through time and space
I see
a lovely shining moment
that we shared in the past

at the time
all I saw was its brevity
its pain, its confusion

now I see
how each instant of time
each touch
each word
truly shone like pure gold

each word a poem
each smile a silent song
each breath a separate silver pleasure

each touch a jewel
you placed against my skin

Since Time Began

I love the ocean
I feel it pulling me
I love its moods and the seagulls crying
I love the crash and the roar
of the waves lapping the shore
pounding on the sand
I love the rhythm of its movements
swaying to some ancient tune
surely it has moved this way
since time began

and I love you
I feel you pulling me to you
I love your moods and your voice in my ear
I love the strength and power of you
and the way you feel
moving slowly against me
I love the rhythm of your movements
surely we have been together
making love like this
since time began

Smiling

ah, my friend,
the others see me smiling at my work.
but it's not my work I'm enjoying.

all day long,
I keep getting flashes of you—
I see your hand reaching for me,
I have a quick memory
of your face so close,
a brief glimpse of your lips opening
to touch mine . . .

ah, I smile at my work . . .

Sorrows

let me drown my sorrows
in you;
let me slide my fingers
up and down
your smooth surfaces.

render me senseless.
do not let me feel pain.
let me drift,
let me float free and easy
and laugh.
let me hide myself
in you
and hold you close.

help me, hide me.
use your magic
to make my mind
all misty around the edges
so my numb brain
cannot feel,
cannot remember,
cannot think ahead
to what might be
or what might never be.

>>>

let me drown my sorrows
in you,
my tall cool glass
of vodka and orange juice,
liquid bliss
like Novocain
smooth, sweet drops
slipping down my throat.

ah, let me forget.
let me be numb and free of pain.

Tangled

I feel
that our futures,
our destinies
are all
tangled up
together

whether
we like it
or not

Together

we are good together,
you and I.
you fill up all my spaces
that are so empty
when you are gone.

Touch the Edge of You

ocean
beautiful powerful ocean
the strength and power of you
frightens me
you put me in my place
make me feel so small
next to you

I want to touch the edge of you
and feel you in my fingers
hold you to the sun
see the light inside you
and dive down deep into you
and know the depths of you

and then there's you
beautiful powerful you
the strength and power of you
frightens me
you make me feel so small
next to you

I want to touch the edge of you
run my fingers over the contours
of your marvelous body
and feel you in my hands
hold you up to the sun
see the light inside you
and dive down deep inside of you
and know you
and know you . . .

Velvet Haze

I can
almost
lose myself
in the pattern
on the curtains

and the stripes
of sunlight
across the floor

sometimes I swear
shafts of my mind
go flying off
to better places
or else
float in a velvet haze
around my body

I feel
such mindless joy
such delicious inexpressible pleasure

lost and alone
inside myself

When You Are Near

I'm afraid
it is written
all over me
in flashing neon letters—
my burning, aching,
desperate desire for you

I'm afraid
the whole world
can see it in my eyes—
my naked need
for you

Your Mark

you have altered
the unmovable mountains
of my mind

you have left
your mark
upon my life

After

My Life

my life
is as empty
as an old deserted house

there is no music
no sound
no laughter

it is creaking in the wind
moved by old memories
the windows are boarded up
by pain
the doors are locked and barred
against everything
and everyone

I will not open up again
I will stay alone
in my safe darkness
I will stay alone
with my sorrow
for companionship
I will not let anyone
hurt me again
like you did

Remembering

I keep remembering the last time
we touched

it haunts me
and it always will

your hands, your voice,
your exciting caresses
lasted only a luscious brief hour or so

we talked, we touched,
we were so close and so warm.
we didn't know
it was the last time

we smiled into each other's eyes.
your hand squeezed mine
and suddenly, simply
you were gone
from my life

Survive

I will survive
though each breath
is another pain

I will survive
though each thought
is another hurt

I am one big bruise
inside and out
I hurt and I want you
so much

Things

I dream of you
now that you are gone

I remember
each touch, each kiss
each lingering, longing look

I remember
things I should have said
but didn't
things I should have done
but couldn't

This Day

it was breathless
in the little clearing
in the new growth of pines
cars hummed not far away
we could clearly see the drivers
they didn't notice us
in the thick trees

we'd made our excuses
carved out a couple of hours
from our real lives

I'd brought a blanket
and a pitcher of screwdrivers
you just brought yourself

it felt dangerous
we felt exposed
here in broad daylight

only the spring sun watched
as sweat glistened on us
as we drank and moved together
tongues and bodies
touching in the age-old dance
absolutely exotic
heightened by the wilderness
the chance of being seen   >>>

no matter the hurt and pain
later caused by us
we wouldn't have missed this day
for anything
remembered, treasured
now that we are older

when all else
is forgotten
we will remember this day

Today

today
I feel
only anger
that we've lost
each other

perhaps tomorrow
I will feel
only the
suffocating sorrow
of my loss

Touch

out in public
lots of people moving

I see you
you see me
as you approach

we can't stop
we don't speak

our eyes don't dare
to meet

but you touch me
as you pass

one knowing finger
runs down my forearm

just lightly brushing
along my skin

your finger moves
with no haste

sliding a white hot path
that I feel everywhere

Wandering Lost

I am here
alone

wandering lost
in the grand canyon

you left
in my heart

Creative Nonfiction

Decisions, Decisions

Shannon kept working, filing, keeping one eye out in the lobby through the big glass window. She never knew when he might come in. God, he turned her on. They had first kissed a couple of weeks ago, told each other how much they liked each other. They were shocked, stunned, horrified at what they felt. They were both married and agreed they did not want to hurt their spouses. But she had never been so excited, never felt so alive. Pierce was a silver-tongued devil—oh, the things he had whispered to her . . .

Shannon had always felt like she had a safe, perfect little life, all planned out. She had met one guy and was going to stay married to him forever. But oh, the pull she felt now—to stray, to touch, to feel and experience the things she had read about in all those damned romance novels.

She looked up again. There he was. Pierce. Even his name turned her on. She caught his eye and they both lit up, unable to keep from smiling broadly. Their looks held. He was well-known and well-liked in town, a successful businessman. Oh, that thick hair and trim beard. What a hunk. If you looked up "hunk" in the dictionary, his picture would be right there. All that dark hair and coffee-rich-with-cream skin—definitely her type. *Good grief.* How could everyone in the place not notice this spark, this intensity? If someone walked between them, they'd surely be badly burned. Moments passed as they eyed each other up and down. A secretary waited on him.

"Shannon." She spun around. Her husband Terry stood in the doorway to the file room, his face pale.

"Oh, uh, hi." Shannon walked toward him. "What are you doing here?"

"We were supposed to meet for lunch." Terry

swallowed, glanced at Pierce. "What's going on?"

"What? Nothing. What do you mean?"

"Shannon, I saw you looking at him." He stepped toward her. "What is going on?"

"What? No. Nothing." Shannon risked a glance at Pierce as she turned to get her purse. He finished with his business, noticed Terry, put his head down, and strode for the door. *Chicken.*

Shannon heaved a sigh, kept her eyes firmly on Terry. "I've had a bad day, dear. I'm a basket case. Take me to lunch."

Lunch was silent. Her salad caught in her throat. Full of lustful thoughts lately, Shannon hadn't been able to eat and pounds had dropped off. Today though, her throat was completely closing up on her. *Oh my god. Poor Terry.* He'd never been a macho man. She knew he loved her beyond words but he always had trouble telling her.

Terry wasn't eating much either. He kept smoothing the few strands of hair across the top of his head. Finally he shoved his plate aside, drank a few swallows from his glass of milk. He took a deep breath, his eyes on the table, and blurted out, "I know I'm not good enough for you, Shannon. But I've tried to be a good husband. What can I do to be better?"

Whoa. He is really worried. That was a long speech for him. Oh, the thoughts she'd had about Pierce, the things she'd wanted to do with him, the things he had said to her, the places in her that he had awakened. She felt like her eyes were floating. Images of the years of marriage with Terry, their kids, trips they'd taken—all of it swamped her. She pulled herself together with an effort. She'd call Pierce tomorrow.

"You can't do anything better, dear. You're the best."

STOLEN HEART

(for R.)

Abstract Painting of My Dark Outlaw

Wrapped like barbed wire around
my heart. His skin, the color of coffee rich
with cream. Across my life like a shooting
star. Deep silences in him. Tracing one fingertip
along my arm and making me shiver. Empty side
of the bed. Dark shadows of his past
haunting his eyes. His slow, lazy smile. That hard
frozen pain he can't outrun. Stars
in his eyes and the wind in his hair. The space
between us keeps growing, a canyon.

The way he reaches for me. Words vibrate
in my heart, low-hung with torment. Dark flashes
of old memories cross his face. Let the light
in his eyes dance. Some unbreakable
tether is still between us. The whimpers
in his sleep. The whole world is out there
calling. When he is eighty and done
running, will he come back to me?

Another Heartbreak

here I am
poised and ready
to fall
as open and vulnerable
as I can be

poised and ready
for another
heartbreak

Are You Sure

you're so determined
to leave me;
you're so sure you want
to be on your way.
are you sure you won't
miss me?
are you sure what we have here
isn't something special?
are you sure you can find someone
out there
who loves you more
than I do?

By My Side

the path through life
would have seemed
so short and sweet
with you next to me

but oh,
the endless length of it,
the countless plodding steps,
with the space beside me
empty

Come Touch Me

trace one fingertip
down my forehead,
along my nose,
touch my lips,
cradle my chin

touch my heart
and feel its wanting

feel in my soul
the desperate sadness

stir in me somewhere
the will and the nerve
to love
again

Dark Flashes

you run to the far edges
of the world
and back again
running from dark flashes
of old memories best forgotten
that streak across your thoughts
unbidden.

when there's nowhere left to run
then you hide in your music.

are you done running now?
have you met them face to face
with my solid love beside you—
is it better now?

geography did not make the difference . . .
love did.

The Empty End of Things

I am really
feeling
the empty end
of things

I see gravity
spoiling
my lines
when once
I felt
beautiful

I feel
my age
my childlessness
the absence
of family

I see
my inability
to change anything

but mostly
I still
just feel
the loss
of you

Heartfull, Hurtful

the day he left,
I bought a pair of earrings—
too expensive—
heart shapes of black and gold.

these hearts won't break,
cold metal studded to my ears—
one heart to replace the one he took,
the other for a spare.

The Hole in My Heart

did I just do the stupidest thing in my life
asking you to leave?

the emptiness—the vastness
of this huge hole
in my heart
takes my breath away

I told myself there were so many reasons
why you should go
and now I cannot remember
one of them

Keep Busy

when I'm not moving,
planning, doing,
crossing things off my list,

loneliness shoulders its way in
next to me and sits down—
a presence nearly as real
as the one
who used to be here.

Looking Back through Years

looking back through years of faces,
feelings, words
I still see your face before all others
clearer than the rest
and nearer, dearer to my heart

as long as you are on this earth
I know I cannot see beyond you

when you are eighty
and done running
will you finally come back to me?
when you have tasted all the world
has to offer
will you finally know that the best part
was what you'd left behind?

will you sit down with me before the fire
and hold my hand
and will you stay, finally?

looking back through years of faces,
feelings, words
I still see your face before all others
clearer than the rest
and nearer, dearer to my heart

Morning Realization

I wake
in the morning,
open my eyes,
remember my name.
the details of my life
come floating to me:
things I must do today,
promises I must keep.
I yawn and stretch
and roll over

to face the lonely pillow—
your side of the bed
empty.

the avalanche hits me then.
I have lost you,
you are gone from my life.
the horror, the realization
settles on me
with a great weight
constricting my heart
and my breathing.

the loss of you
forgotten for a moment
in my dreams . . .

Observations

mirrored in the ruffled river beside me,
horses eating up the sky of clouds—
cantering, churning with long strides,
chewing up their path, the ribbons of color.

my face, my eyes, look back at me—
watch me eat up my future
in great gulps
turning it into my past so fast.

my body, not yet infirm, but not firm either,
can't carry my burdens, real or not—
and my heart—too small to hold
its load of grief.

Over and Over

I reach for you over and over
like I did on our first night
together—
you were always there
rising under my hand
turning to me
both of us
slick with sweat

how good it felt
to be young and beautiful
to know we were desired

the lovemaking
was so easy then
when muscles responded
when bodies didn't ache

I reach for you over and over
like I did on our first night
together—
my aching fingers
finding only
the empty side
of the bed

Parallel Life

I am sure that
I must also
be living somewhere else
in a universe parallel
to this make-believe life

another life
where I am
really
more important to you
than the bars

where we live
and love
exquisitely

and nothing
will ever
separate us

a place where
we are living
the life
we were supposed
to live

Roses

the roses
you sent me
lasted five days—
you stayed
with me for
nine days—

but the love
you started
in my heart
could last
through
one hundred lifetimes . . .

The Same Stars

I am
so far from home,
so far from everything
that is safe and secure.

what a relief
to look up to the night sky,
to see the familiar faces of the stars,
the same constellations,
the same sky.

I am not lost
after all.

Shooting Star

you are a beautiful dream
that brightened up my life
like a shooting star
so brief, so lovely, so unexpected

your image remains
permanently burned in my memory
sliding a white fluorescent path
across my thoughts
like a meteor flashing across
a night sky

So Far Away

there you are again
staring silently
out the window

looking longingly
down the road
to freedom.

you are still here,
alive and warm
in my arms
but your mind,
your soul
have traveled
so far away.

why can't you
be happy
just to be
here with me?

Space Man

the space between us
keeps growing
ever widening
like a flooded river
in the spring

and though I think
I know you
I cannot foresee or
figure out
your next move

you need your space
you said
you needed time
to yourself

but then why
did I lose you
the one time
I gave you space
the one time
you were not
the center
of my world
for a little while

I had been right
to stay close
to keep no more space
between us
than air to breathe

The Stars Move

the days pass me by,
another weekend comes

the earth turns
and the sun rolls by
and the clouds float past
and storms come
and seasons go

and the stars move
and another year is gone

I am still here
and it seems that
I'm always going to love you

whether you have
the sense to be with me
or not

Still Here

you left me
but you couldn't really leave
not totally

we were so close
for so long
two hearts in such synchronicity
that now we are still
a part of each other's lives

much the same
as a spouse or parent
who has died
still lingers close

only slightly beneath
our consciousness
and always
just behind our closed eyelids
in sleep

Things I Fear

I dread winter, snow, icy roads
I hate the fear in my heart

I fear falling on ice
broken bones hiding
beneath a dust of snow
becoming dependent on others
having no say in my future

I hate cruel women, their snarky words
I hate weak men who fall for their charms

I fear falling for someone
broken hearts hiding
behind a handsome face
becoming another casualty
having no say in my future

A Treasured Moment

here is a treasured moment
when he lets me into his heart.
they are so few
and far between.

usually he teases me,
he provokes me,
he laughs and jokes
and won't take life seriously.

but, once in a while—a treasured moment
unguarded, when he lets me in—
he tells me a vivid word picture
of some beautiful thing he saw today.
his real being is clear to me
as he speaks from his depths.

for just a short space of time,
he gives me a treasured moment
and lets me into his heart.

Wasted Time

I spend too much time alone,
rattling around in this house,
too much time in my mind,
spinning around in my head.

I work all day
so separate from people,
not wanting to absorb their troubles,
trying to wall myself off.

I come home, feed pets,
TV on for company,
writing my sorrows down,
spilling out my loneliness.

then confused, lost,
off balance, off to bed,
still searching through my dreams
for some sign of you.

Will You Know?

when I die,
will you know?

somewhere far away,
will you turn
from what you are doing?
will you wonder
what
you felt

when I touch you,
sliding by
on my way
to forever?

You Ask

you ask me if I love you . . .
how can I reply
so that you will
fully understand . . .

I will try to fold my meager words
around you;
I will try to draw you
a word picture
so that I can show you
the magnitude
of my caring . . .

a drop of water in the ocean
is what I felt for anyone
in my past.

what I feel for you
is the whole ocean.

Creative Nonfiction

Another Life

The Mardi Gras beads, gold and purple, hung from his rear view mirror. I tried to focus on something else, but as his truck moved and swayed over the bumps in my driveway, the beads flicked cruel shards of sunlight into my eyes.

He was here with me today and we were off to spend some time together, but they were short hours. It would be a brief respite from my loneliness since he moved out.

Those beads on the rear view mirror clacked with mean laughter in my ears. Where had he gotten them? Had some other girl worn them and left them with him? What a slap in the face. What a nasty reminder that he had another life, that he wasn't mine any longer.

I wanted to ask, but I wouldn't. A cold lump in my throat, either anger or regret, kept me silent. I felt him glance at me, so I summoned my normal beaming smile and flashed it his way. After all, I had another life too, or at least he could think so. We were going to have a great day together and laugh a lot. We were. I was happy to be here. I was.

Another Person's Memories

The old house is still standing. Every year or so, when I drive by it, I think it will be gone, flattened by wind or storm or perhaps just by the strength of me wanting it gone.

I grew up here, brought up by my grandparents. I still dream of the house, still wake up sweating, sobbing, trying to run but unable to.

I left here at sixteen and went as far as I could from our Midwestern town till the ocean stopped me. I spent years trying to forget the things that happened in that house and the surrounding woods. For years I drank too much and tried nearly every drug there was, trying to forget, trying to get farther away.

There were good things in the house too. The hot, lazy days and sleeping on the porch on the summer nights. I had many pets. I went fishing. I swam in a nearby lake. I helped bring cows home from pasture, the drone of grasshoppers loud in my ears, swatting mosquitoes and deer flies. There were many chores to do, animals to care for, kittens and calves to love.

I remember the huge fields, the tall green grass murmuring in the wind, laying down on my back—seeing only sky above the waving greenness around me. I wished that was all I had to think about, to worry about, wished that everything else was gone but the summer day's heat and the sky far above me, nothing touching me but good things.

Mindful Meal

It was Friday evening after a long week. I came home dog-tired and just wanted a cat-nap. My dog and cat met me at the door and demanded to be fed. I was tired, too tired to be on my feet any longer. My poor aging cat has trouble seeing and I spooned tuna pate into his dish on the counter and made sure he found it. He prefers to just lick the gravy off his food but there is no gravy on pate. *Sorry, kitty.* The young dog was a dancing fool as usual and, after letting her out and back in, I poured some dry food in her dish. She was really irritating.

I was hungry, too. My nap would have to wait. I had decided to fix my favorite simple meal: scrambled eggs with cheese on toast. I had been thinking about it as I fed my pets, anticipating the warm gush of butter and the melded flavors. I broke open two eggs into a bowl and swirled them together with a fork. As they cooked in the microwave, I put two slices of whole grain oat-nut bread in the toaster. This was such good soft bread. When it was done, lightly browned, I covered it with soft organic butter. I like to have the butter pressed down into the bread, completely melted.

As I traversed my kitchen, the dog stayed underfoot, following me, wheeling around me as I moved. She was definitely irritating. I admitted to myself that I envied her for the easy way her muscles moved. When the eggs were done, I salted them and spread the little omelet over one slice of toast and covered it with the other. Then I cut it into two triangles. I loved to make sandwiches out of my meals. I've even been known to make a sandwich out of macaroni and cheese.

I sat down with my egg sandwich and my cup of skim milk and I dug in. The cat was now done eating and he moseyed over from the other end of the counter to sit near my plate. He just isn't himself these days—not showing any interest in my food and not much in his. He just stays near me for the company. I know he won't be with me much longer. The air rumbled with his purrs. The dog sat on the floor, eyes glued to every bite I took. I never feed her people food; I don't know why she does this. Can't she unlearn this habit?

My sandwich was hot as I bit into it. The house was cold and I appreciated this small comfort of a hot meal. A little organic butter dripped down onto my plate and I made sure to wipe it up with my next bite of sandwich. The eggs were soft and the toast had crunchy bits of nuts in it. With the oatmeal and the butter, it had a great flavor and I closed my eyes in pleasure. *Oh, drat!* I had forgotten to put in the cheese. That always added more pleasure. Too late now. I made sure to mop up every bit of egg or butter or toast crumbs from the plate. I left some of the crusts just because I could.

I remembered when my sweetheart was with me. We'd fix a meal together, bumping hips in the small kitchen. Cooking was fun then. He always had unique ideas for meals. It's no fun cooking for one. I seemed to fix the same three or four things over and over.

I put my lonely plate and the egg bowl and my silverware into the sink and headed to the couch for my nap.

Now I Can Feel

I am a person who sticks to things. I am consistent and persistent, always. I hold jobs for twenty-plus years and I have lived in the same place my whole life.

I was disdainful of those silly unsettled people who flit from job to job, who move from place to place. And I grew up thinking that you needed to choose one person and spend your whole life with them—that's the way is should be.

After a divorce and some break-ups, I now allow myself to realize that each new person in your life has something to bring to you, something you need to learn from them. I know there is a reason they came into your life. And I can actually see that perhaps a change of home or job is okay and acceptable.

Finally, I have stretched my mental boundaries and I can get a glimmering of the reasons why people move about, why people crave change in their lives, why people need the newness of arriving and the comfort of departing.

I can feel the unrest beneath my surfaces.

Weekend River Walk

The sun and the wind tickle the leaves and reach through to scatter dark and light. The long evening shadows send fingers of shade reaching across the river to the waving grass on the riverbank.

Two people stroll along the river, taking their habitual weekend walk. There was a time out walking that they always had to touch each other, arm in arm, an arm slung over shoulders, or hands held.

She wonders what he will say or if, as usual, he will just be silent. She will have to bring it up—his absences, the missing hours. It can't all be work. Her throat closes on the words. Why doesn't he touch her anymore? She aches for him, to have him reach for her. She feels empty and wonders when things changed.

He wonders why she never talks to him anymore. When he comes home, exhausted, she turns her back. He wants to tell her about his day, needs her encouragement for a job that is draining him. She is angry about something and he doesn't know what. He is afraid to reach for her hand now, not sure of her response. He feels lost and wonders when things changed.

They walk on, with similar thoughts locked in separate minds, hearts hardening, into the deepening shadows. They follow the musical curve of the river that they don't see or hear.

P.S.
I still love you
both.

www.ingramcontent.com/pod-product-compliance
Lightning Source LLC
Chambersburg PA
CBHW060355050426
42449CB00009B/1751